A Year of Fun
JUST for FIVE'S

By Theodosia Spewock

Fun seasonal activities, songs,
poems, and fingerplays—
plus practical advice
for parents

Illustrated by
Susan Dahlman

TOTLINE® BOOKS

Warren Publishing House, Inc.

Introduction

Welcome to the world of the 5-year-old. It may be hard to believe that your child is already 5 years old. The preschool years seem to have flown by quickly. Very soon your child will begin a new and exciting period in life: going to school!

Just for Five's has been designed to help you understand the characteristics of the typical 5-year-old. Just turn to the appropriate month and begin! The activities can be completed in any sequence and repeated as often as you like. *Just for Five's* includes a "readiness checklist" that describes skills your child will need to be familiar with in order to continue to learn and grow in kindergarten.

The stages of development you will read about are based on the average 5-year-old child. It is important to remember that no two children are alike. Therefore, don't be alarmed if your child does not yet exhibit all the skills described in *Just for Five's*, because young children mature at different rates.

Please remember that your love, encouragement, and praise will help make school a rewarding and gratifying experience for your child. Show your 5-year-old that you are proud of his or her accomplishments at home and in school.

We wish you and your child an exciting year of learning and growing.

Have fun!

Typical Behavior of Five's

Parents need to understand that every child is an individual and that not all children behave alike. Some children reach the customary stages of development at the appropriate time, while others may experience them sooner or much later. The following section describes some of the typical behaviors that a 5-year-old child might exhibit. You may observe that your child exhibits some, all, or none of these behaviors.

The 5-Year-Old

Most 5-year-olds:

- share with others.
- are able to make friends with children.
- enjoy participating in games.
- enjoy music.
- love being read to and talked to by adults.
- are able to request help with a frustrating or difficult activity.
- are able to dress and clean themselves.
- are curious and eager to please parents and teachers.
- find it difficult, at times, to admit wrongdoing.
- complain of aching heads, stomachs, ears, faces, or feet when overexcited.

Kindergarten Readiness

The following is a list of skills that your child should be familiar with before he or she starts kindergarten. Don't be concerned if your child has not mastered all of the skills before starting school, because kindergarten is the time when your child will be concentrating on these and more readiness skills to enable him or her to succeed as he or she progresses through school.

- recognizes and prints his or her name
- identifies six or more colors
- identifies basic shapes such as circles, squares, triangles, rectangles, and diamonds
- counts to 10
- gives first name, address, and telephone number
- listens and follows simple directions
- cuts with scissors
- plays cooperatively with others
- speaks in complete sentences
- shows independence in ways such as washing and dressing and toileting skills
- understands concepts such as in/out, up/down, big/little, over/under, same/different, left/right, and before/after
- completes simple tasks
- classifies common objects into categories such as animals, food, toys, and shapes
- stays with one activity for 10 to 12 minutes

♠♠♠ Totline. Fun For

JANUARY

New Year's Collage

Let your child make "confetti" by punching circles out of construction paper with a hole punch. Have him or her brush glue all over a full sheet of construction paper and drop strands of silver tinsel and handfuls of the confetti on top of the glue. Let dry and hang up for everyone to admire.

Shape Concentration

Cut eight index cards in half. On each pair of halves draw a different shape (square, triangle, circle, or rectangle). Mix up the cards, spread them face down on a flat surface, and take turns with your child selecting two cards. If the shapes match, keep them. If they do not match, turn them face down and continue taking turns.

Raw and Cooked

Before steaming sliced vegetables or adding them to soup, talk with your child about the taste and texture of vegetables that are raw. Later, compare the taste and texture of the same vegetables after they've been cooked.

Jumping Beans

Pretend that you and your child are jumping beans as you both stand on pieces of construction paper that represent plates. Turn on the music and begin jumping up and down without falling off your plates. Vary the speed of the music and your jumping.

Shoe Box Dollhouse

Use a shoe box to make a dollhouse by placing it on one of its long sides. Use glue and pieces of wallpaper or patterned wrapping paper to help your child decorate the walls. Color the floor with crayons or use paper to make carpets. Cut pictures of furniture and people from catalogs and glue them to small empty thread spools to make them stand. Have fun arranging the furniture and people in different ways.

Bird Treat

Help your child use a table knife to spread peanut butter all over a pine cone. Then roll the pine cone in birdseed. Use a piece of yarn to hang it outside for the birds to enjoy.

Number Cans

Cover five empty frozen-juice concentrate cans with construction paper. Number the cans from one to five by drawing on dots with a felt-tip marker. Set out 15 craft sticks or plastic drinking straws. Help your child count the numbers of dots on the cans and place the appropriate number of sticks or straws inside them.

Time Line

On a long piece of paper, draw a long horizontal line. Write the date of your child's birth at the beginning of the line. Then talk with your child about important events in his or her life and mark them at the appropriate places on the time line. If desired, attach actual photos of the event or let your child illustrate the events.

Dancing Paper Clip

Fill a jar with water and drop a steel paper clip in it. Tell your child that you can make the paper clip dance up and down in the water without touching it. Then move a magnet up and down outside the jar to make the clip dance. Let your child try it. Explain that the magnetic force from the magnet passes through the glass and water to make the clip move.

Simple Snowflakes

Show your child how to fold a coffee filter in half and then in half again. Help him or her cut small triangles out of the folded edges (be sure to tell your child to leave a little room between each triangle). Then have him or her unfold the filter to see the snowflake.

Frosty Pictures

Ask your child to draw a winter outdoor scene on a piece of construction paper. Make a solution of half Epsom salts and half water. Let your child paint over the picture with the mixture. As it dries, your child will notice sparkling crystals begin to form.

Salt Box

Cut black construction paper to fit inside the bottom of a shallow box. Tape it in place. Cover the bottom of the box with a layer of salt. Show your child how to use a finger to draw letters found in his or her name in the salt. Show how the letters can be erased by gently shaking the box from side to side.

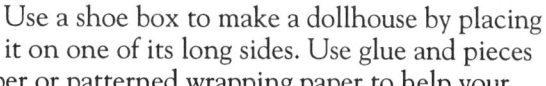

When Friends Visit
Hot or Cold

Have the children sit in a circle and take turns selecting one child to be It. This child will close his or her eyes as you hide a small object in the room. Then have the child who is It look for the hidden object. When the child gets close to the object, have the other children say "hot." When the child gets farther away, say "cold." Continue until the object is found.

Special Day Celebration
National Soup Month

When winter winds blow, nothing tastes better than a bowl of hot soup. Choose any day during January for your celebration. Talk to your child about favorite kinds of soups and how they are prepared. Read the story *Stone Soup*, and make "Stone Soup" for your family.

Stone Soup

Pour 2 quarts chicken or beef broth into a large pot and have your child put in a round, smooth stone that has been scrubbed and boiled. Add chopped carrots, celery, potatoes, onions, zucchini, and tomatoes. Bring to a boil. Then cover and simmer for about 1 hour. Add seasoning to taste.

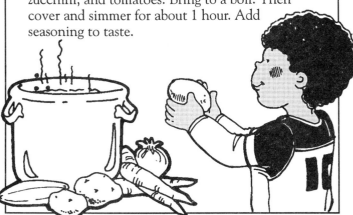

Manners

Sung to: *"Hickory, Dickory, Dock"*

Cover your mouth when you cough.
Cover your mouth when you sneeze.
If you cough or if you sneeze,
Cover your mouth, if you please.

Ruth Miller

Fine-Motor Development

Five-year-olds are becoming more coordinated when using their fingers and hands. They are proud that they are learning to tie their shoes and color pictures inside the lines. Promote fine-motor development by encouraging your 5-year-old to:

- brush his or her teeth.
- use crayons, pencils, and markers.
- cut with scissors.
- play with clay, mud, sand, and water.
- assemble puzzles.
- sew with large plastic needles, yarn, and burlap.
- trace objects using stencils.
- help prepare food by mixing, pouring, stirring, measuring, and rolling.
- sort hardware such as nails, screws, and bolts.
- make necklaces and bracelets by stringing O-shaped cereal or macaroni.
- pick up cotton balls and other small objects with tongs.
- zip and button.
- buckle seat belts.
- fingerpaint.
- draw circles, squares, and triangles.
- trace shapes, letters, and numerals.
- dress and undress without assistance.
- use a hole punch.

♠♠♠ Totline® Fun For

FEBRUARY

Letter Cups

Print a different upper-case alphabet letter in the bottom of six paper baking cups. Place the cups in a muffin tin. Print the same upper-case letters on small circles cut from construction paper. Have your child sort the circles into the appropriate muffin-tin cups.

Sack Stories

Place several small toys or objects in a paper sack. Start telling a simple story. Then take turns with your child and family members in choosing an object from the sack, holding it up, and incorporating it into your story. Continue until all of the objects have been used.

Dot-to-Dot Patterns

Draw simple dot-to-dot patterns (straight, wavy, jagged lines) across a sheet of paper. Draw a large dot on the left side of each pattern to indicate where to begin. Show your child how to connect the dots with a marker or crayon by starting at the large dots and progressing to the right. This activity reinforces left-to-right progression.

Problem Solving

Ask "What if?" questions to help your child come up with positive solutions to sharing problems that commonly arise. For example, ask, "What if you want to play on the swing but your brother won't get off? What if there's one cookie left and both you and your sister want it? What if you're starting a game and you and a friend both want to be first?"

Find the Queen of Hearts

From a deck of cards, select the queen of and two other cards. Place the cards face up on the table. Turn the cards face down and move them around. Ask your child to turn over the card he or she thinks is the queen of hearts. Reverse roles and continue playing.

Magic Hearts

Help your child brush white vinegar on a sheet of white construction paper. Then cover the paper with small hearts that have been cut from red tissue paper. As the vinegar dries, the tissue paper hearts will fall off, leaving red heart prints.

Heart Hop

Cut large heart shapes out of construction paper and tape them to the floor around the room. Then turn on some music and join your child in hopping from heart to heart.

Family Album

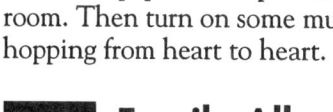

Help your child draw a picture of each person in your family, using a separate sheet of paper for each person. Collect magazine pictures, food labels, pieces of colored paper, etc., and put them in a box. Give your child one of the family members' pictures. Help him or her select items from the box that represent that person's favorite color, food, activity, and so on. Glue them to that person's picture. Repeat with the remaining pictures. Use fabric to make a decorative cover. Secure the sheets together using staples or a hole punch and yarn. Find a place of honor for the book with other family albums.

Valentine Placemat

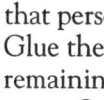

Cut two identical placemat-size rectangles out of clear self-stick paper. Remove the backing from one of the rectangles. Help your child arrange hearts cut from pink, red, and white tissue paper onto the sticky side of the rectangle. Add sparkle by sprinkling on glitter. Remove the backing from the second rectangle and carefully place it sticky side down over the decorated rectangle. Trim off any overhanging edges.

Air Painting

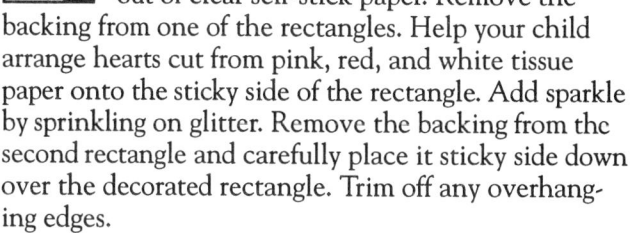

Give your child a straw and a piece of paper. Spoon a little watered-down tempera paint onto the piece of paper. Let your child blow through the straw to move the paint around on the paper and create designs.

Floating Heart Art

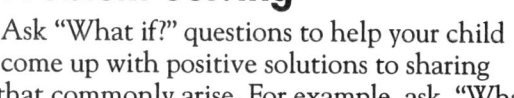

Cut heart shapes out of pink construction paper. Fill a dishpan with water. Help your child grate red and white chalk into powder and then sprinkle a little powder on top of the water in the dishpan. Let your child gently place a heart shape on top of the sprinkled chalk. Carefully lift each heart shape out of the water and place it on a flat surface to dry.

When Friends Visit
Puzzle Pals

Separate the pieces of a puzzle into two piles. Give one pile to your child and the other pile to his or her friend. To assemble the puzzle, have the children take turns selecting pieces from their piles.

Cold Winds

When cold winds blow

And bring us snow,
(Hug self and shiver.)

At night what I like most

Is to crawl in bed
(Pretend to climb in bed.)

And hide my head,

And sleep as warm as toast.
*(Pretend to pull up covers,
then close eyes.)*

Adapted Traditional

Why Should Parents Read to Their Children?

One of the most important things you can do as a parent is to read to your child. The time you spend reading to your child can influence his or her attitude toward books and affect the success he or she will have when learning to read. When children listen to stories they learn:

- new words and ideas.
- that the stories they listen to come from the "black marks" (print) on each page.
- that a book starts at the front and continues through the pages to the back.
- that print is read across the page from left to right.

Special Day Celebration
George Washington's Birthday

February 22 is the birthday of George Washington, a famous general, our first president, and the "Father of Our Country." To celebrate this event, visit the public library with your child and find a story about young George and the cherry tree.

Be My Valentine

Sung to: *"Mary Had a Little Lamb"*

You're a special friend of mine,
Friend of mine, friend of mine.
You're a special friend of mine.
Be my valentine!

Jean Warren

Valentine Tarts

Help your child roll out refrigerator biscuits into 3-inch circles. Spread each one with margarine and strawberry jam. Help your child fold each biscuit over to make a tart. Use a fork to seal the edges together. Bake according to package directions. Serve warm with a glass of milk.

✳✳✳ Totline® Fun For
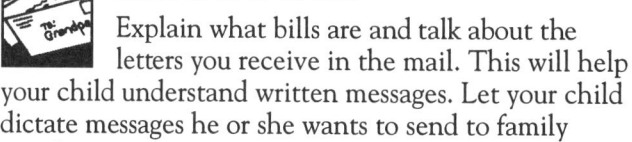 MARCH

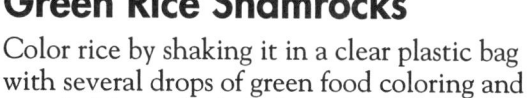 Peanut Toss

Cut a large circle, a square, and a triangle out of the bottom of a sturdy cardboard box. Place the box (shapes side up) on the floor. Join your child in trying to toss unshelled peanuts into the box through the shapes.

Green Rice Shamrocks

Color rice by shaking it in a clear plastic bag with several drops of green food coloring and several drops of rubbing alcohol. Spread the rice on paper towels to dry. Help your child brush diluted glue onto a shamrock shape cut from white posterboard. Then sprinkle green rice all over the glue.

My Special Box

Help your child transform a shoe box into a special container by decorating it with wrapping paper, markers, stickers, glitter, etc. Let your child use the box for keeping his or her private, special things.

Water Garbage

Sometimes plastic ring-type holders found on six-packs of aluminum cans can end up in the water where fish and other animals that live there get caught in them. Help your child make these holders less hazardous by using scissors to cut through each ring in the holder before throwing it away.

Learning Through Touch

Cut plastic straws into small pieces of various lengths. Ask your child to close his or her eyes. Then place a straw section in each hand and ask your child to tell by touch which section is the shortest and which is the longest. Take turns playing this game.

 Sprouting Shamrocks

Cut a shamrock shape out of terrycloth. Place the shape in an aluminum pie tin and add a little water. Help your child sprinkle alfalfa seeds all over the shamrock. Place the pie tin in a sunny spot and regularly add water to keep the shape moist. Observe over the next week as the seeds sprout and turn the shamrock green.

 Read the Mail

Explain what bills are and talk about the letters you receive in the mail. This will help your child understand written messages. Let your child dictate messages he or she wants to send to family members.

 Peanut Transfer

Join your child in using a pair of small kitchen tongs to place unshelled peanuts in each compartment of an ice-cube tray. How many peanuts fit in each compartment?

 Stop, Drop, and Roll

Talk to your child about how to stop, drop, and roll if his or her clothes ever catch fire. Together, run in place. Then at a given signal, stop running, drop to the floor, and roll over and over until the pretend flames are out.

 Writing in Shaving Cream

Spray shaving cream onto a baking sheet. Let your child spread it out and enjoy finger-painting with it. Show your child how to use his or her pointer finger to draw letters that are in his or her name.

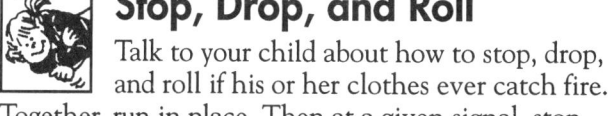 Making a Windsock

Cut the top and bottom off of a round oatmeal container. Cut construction paper to fit around the box. Let your child decorate the paper with felt-tip markers. Glue the paper to the outside of the box. Tape or staple 6-inch strips of crepe paper streamers around the inside bottom edge of the box. To make a hanger for the windsock, punch four holes in the top of the box, lace a string knotted at one end through each hole, and tie the four loose ends together.

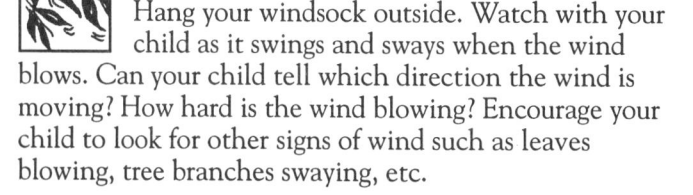 Wind Watching

Hang your windsock outside. Watch with your child as it swings and sways when the wind blows. Can your child tell which direction the wind is moving? How hard is the wind blowing? Encourage your child to look for other signs of wind such as leaves blowing, tree branches swaying, etc.

When Friends Visit
Leprechaun Gold Hunt

Hide gold-colored objects (jewelry, keys, pens, hair clips, etc.) around the room. Set out a large black pot and encourage the children to "help the leprechaun fill his pot with gold" by searching for the hidden objects and placing them in the pot.

Let's Wear Green
Sung to: *"The Mulberry Bush"*

Let's wear green and dance a jig,
Dance a jig, dance a jig.
Let's wear green and dance a jig
On St. Patrick's Day.
All join hands and circle round,
Circle round, circle round.
All join hands and circle round
On St. Patrick's Day.

Jean Warren

Special Celebration
National Peanut Month

March is the time to honor the peanut and its most popular product, peanut butter. Celebrate this month by eating, counting, tossing, and hunting for peanuts. Make homemade peanut butter by combining 2 to 3 tablespoons vegetable oil with 1 cup peanuts and grinding in a blender. Add more oil as needed.

Shamrock Shakes

In a blender container, combine 1 cup chocolate-chip mint ice cream and 1 cup milk. Blend until smooth. Pour into clear plastic cups. Makes 2 to 3 small servings.

Leprechaun Surprise Pudding

Spoon ready-made vanilla pudding into a small bowl. Add one drop of yellow food coloring and one drop of blue. Have your child stir the pudding with a spoon and observe what happens. Your child will enjoy eating the surprise treat.

Language

The language skills of the typical 5-year-old are well developed. Children at this age enjoy talking about a wide variety of subjects. They are constantly learning new words and love using big words when they speak. Most have a vocabulary of about 2,000 words and can speak in sentences six to seven words in length. They use speech sounds correctly with the possible exceptions of V, TH, Z, J, and Y.

It is important that parents encourage their children to express themselves through language. This can be done in a variety of ways. Children practice and learn new language by:

- singing songs.
- listening to stories.
- telling jokes.
- conversing with adults and other children.
- retelling stories that were read to them.
- answering the telephone.
- playing with puppets.
- asking questions.
- describing events of the day.
- reciting nursery rhymes, simple poems, and fingerplays.
- describing or making up stories from pictures in books or magazines.

✦✦✦ Totline® Fun For

APRIL

Letter Detective

Choose an alphabet letter such as B. Print B's and other letters on separate self-stick notes and place them around the room where your child can find them easily. Give your child a magnifying glass. Instruct your child to search for the B's and bring them back to you. Take turns being the Letter Detective.

Mystery Egg

Hide a small familiar object inside a plastic egg. Have your child shake the egg and guess what is inside. Then give clues about the object (its color, how it is used, etc.). When the object has been identified, let your child open the egg. Take turns playing this game.

Bunny Counters

Draw a large bunny shape on each of five index cards. Number the cards from 1 to 5. Set out glue and cotton balls. Help your child select one card at a time, identify the numeral on it, and then glue that many cotton balls onto the bunny. Display your child's creations.

Coupon Book

Staple several coupons together. Encourage your child to "read" the Coupon Book by looking at the pictures and naming the products. Choose a numeral or letter and let your child search for and circle it throughout the Coupon Book.

Bunny Afoot

Trace around your child's foot on a piece of white paper and cut out the foot shape. Position the foot shape vertically with the narrow end at the top. (This will be the head.) Help your child cut ears, whiskers, eyes, and paws out of colored construction paper and then glue them onto the foot shape. Add a cotton-ball tail.

Silly Mixed-Up Creatures

Cut pictures of people and animals from magazines. Then cut the pictures in half to make "tops" and "bottoms." Place the tops in one pile and the bottoms in another. Have your child create Silly Mixed-Up Creatures by mixing the tops and bottoms and gluing them onto construction paper.

Egg Toss

Take turns with your child tossing plastic eggs into a large basket or a box. If desired, place a pillow in the container to cut down on noise.

Marble Painting

Cut a piece of light-colored paper to fit in the bottom of a baking dish. Place three or four large dabs of different colors of tempera paint on the paper. Let your child place two or three marbles in the dish and tip it back and forth to create a marble painting.

Tiptoe Through the Tulips

On the floor, arrange "tulips" cut from construction paper. Join your child in tiptoeing through the tulips without stepping on them.

No-Mess Fingerpainting

Spoon 1 tablespoon each of blue and yellow finger paint into a resealable plastic bag. Squeeze the air out of the bag and seal it. Give the bag to your child and let him or her "fingerpaint" on the surface of the bag.

Spoon Mirror

Give your child a shiny spoon. Let your child find his or her reflection on the back of the spoon. Have your child move the spoon up and down and back and forth. What happens to the reflection? Have your child look into the front of the spoon. What happens to the reflection now?

Making a Rainbow

Place a small mirror in a clear glass of water and tilt it against the side of the glass. Stand the glass in a window in direct sunlight. Can your child find a rainbow? (If not, tilt the mirror a little until the rainbow appears on a wall.)

Daffy Daffodil

Help your child flatten a yellow paper baking cup. Spread glue on the center portion. Then place a white cupcake liner upright on top of the glue to make a daffodil flower. Use a craft stick or a straw for a stem.

When Friends Visit
Camping Out With Books

Cover an old card table with sheets, blankets, or pieces of fabric. Place big, fluffy pillows inside the "tent." Let the children use the space for a "camp-out" reading hideaway.

Special Day Celebration
Earth Day

April 22 is Earth Day. People across the country celebrate this day by wearing green, planting trees, and learning how to use resources wisely. As you discuss Earth Day with your child, have him or her name some activities he or she would like to do such as turning off lights, planting flower seeds, or recycling paper and aluminum cans. Then make a chart that lists those activities down the left side, with the days of the week across the top. Each day, have your child put an X by the activities he or she does.

Healthy Teeth Experiment

Show your child an eggshell. Explain that it is made of calcium, just like our teeth. Set out a glass of cola (with sugar) and a glass of juice. Place part of an eggshell in each glass. Leave another part out. Predict with your child what might happen. After two days, examine the eggshells. (The shells in juice and cola are stained and more brittle than the shell left out.) Discuss the importance of dental hygiene and eating healthful foods.

Keep an eye on your children as they brush their teeth to make sure they don't swallow toothpaste. Fruit-flavored toothpaste is especially tasty to children, and they may be tempted to swallow it. There's no danger in swallowing small amounts of toothpaste, but fluoride can cause tooth discoloration if swallowed in large amounts.

Feelings Face Toast

Help your child spread peanut butter on several slices of toast. Talk about feelings. Place raisins on the toast to make different faces (happy, sad, mad, etc.).

Rainbow Kebabs

Create delicious kebabs by helping your child place a strawberry, an orange segment, a pineapple chunk, a honeydew melon ball (or a green grape), a blueberry, and a purple grape on a bamboo skewer. Talk about the colors of the rainbow as you eat the colorful snacks. (Use vanilla yogurt as a dip.)

Rainbow Colors
Sung to: "Hush, Little Baby"

Rainbow purple, rainbow blue,
Rainbow green and yellow, too.
Rainbow orange, rainbow red,
Rainbow shining overhead.

Jean Warren

Paint-Chip Fun

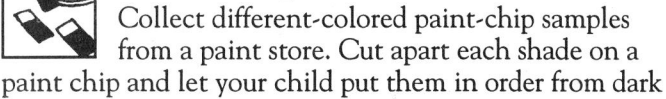

Collect different-colored paint-chip samples from a paint store. Cut apart each shade on a paint chip and let your child put them in order from dark to light.

Basket Weaving

Give your child a plastic berry basket and thin construction-paper strips in several colors. Be sure to cut the strips so that they fit through the spaces in the basket. Help your child weave the paper strips through the spaces to make a colorful woven basket.

Pet-Care Chart

If your family has a pet, talk with your child about the things you must do for it every day. Make a chart listing these tasks. (Draw pictures if desired.) Display the chart in an appropriate place. Each day, check off the tasks on the chart with your child as you complete them together.

Spring Cleaning

Spruce up a favorite outdoor area by cleaning up litter or other odds and ends that have accumulated over the winter. When you are done, let your child plant some flowers, shrubs, or saplings.

Appreciating Nature

Take your child out for a walk to enjoy the fresh smells of spring. Name the different things you smell as you sniff the spring breezes (flowers, damp soil, grass, etc.).

Shapely Creations

Cut construction paper into rectangles, squares, diamonds, circles, triangles, ovals, and semicircles. Help your child arrange these shapes on white paper to make objects, people, and animals. Glue the shapes in place. Add features and background with crayons and felt-tip markers.

Writing Fun

Cover the bottom of a baking pan with a layer of salt or sand. Let your child "write" in the salt or sand with his or her fingers, sticks, straws, unsharpened pencils, etc.

Lovely Lilacs

Cut purple and white tissue paper into 2-inch squares. Show your child how to twist a paper square around a chopstick or the eraser end of a pencil to make a lilac blossom. After your child has made several blossoms, show him or her how to glue the blossoms to craft sticks to make lilac branches. Put the lilacs into the homemade woven basket (activity at left) for a springtime centerpiece.

Pet-Store Visit

Visit a pet store with your child. Talk about the different animals and pet supplies that are on display. Ask a clerk to explain the kinds of care that the animals need every day. Which pets require the most care? The least care?

Mother's Day Cards

Discuss tasks your child could do around the house to help out Mom. Then have him or her make hand prints on three or four sheets of paper. Staple the papers together with a cover on which you have written "Happy Mother's Day." Then let your child decorate the cover and sign his or her name. When she needs a helping hand, Mom can tear out a page and present it to the child. This idea works great for Father's Day as well.

Say Cheese

Give your child a toy to hold such as a teddy bear. Using an old camera, pretend to snap pictures of your child as you give directions for different poses. For example, say, "Move backward one step. Take two steps forward. Stand next to the teddy bear. Hold the bear over your head."

Tipping the Scales

Cut the middle section out of the bottom part of a wire coat hanger. Cover the two sharp ends with masking tape and bend them slightly upward. Punch two holes in the rim of each of two paper cups. Make a handle for each cup by tying on a 6-inch piece of string. Hang the cups from the cut ends of the coat hanger. To use the scale, place a small object (a penny or a crayon) in each cup. Balance the coat hanger scale on a doorknob. Ask your child which object is the heaviest or the lightest. Repeat with other small objects.

When Friends Visit
Let's Find Our Shoes

Collect one shoe from each child. While the children wait out of sight, hide the shoes around the room. When you are ready, call out, "One, two, buckle your shoe!" Let the children look for their shoes. Encourage them to cooperate and help one another find and put on their shoes.

Sunshine Shakes

Place one can (6 ounces) unsweetened frozen orange-juice concentrate, ¾ cup milk, ¾ cup water, 1 teaspoon vanilla, and 6 ice cubes in a blender and blend until smooth and frothy. Pour into small cups. Makes 6 small servings.

Gross-Motor Development

Five-year-olds enjoy play and movement. Activities such as running, jumping, skipping, and climbing are much easier for them because their gross-motor skills (use of arms and legs) are better developed at this age. Children build their self-confidence as they practice these skills.

It is important that parents encourage their youngsters to participate in activities that strengthen muscle control. These include:

- dancing
- hopping on one foot
- jumping rope
- climbing
- exercising
- riding a bicycle with training wheels
- roller skating
- using child-size stilts
- learning to swim
- marching to music
- throwing a ball underhand
- catching a ball or a beanbag
- kicking or bouncing a ball

Special Day Celebration
National Pet Week

The first week in May has been designated as the time for honoring pets. Make a pet collage with your child. Let your child offer to walk one of your neighbors' pets. Take your child to a pet store and enjoy looking at all the animals. Talk about how pets need a lot of love, and then put your child in charge of making sure your pet gets enough love each day. Make the pet-care chart described above.

Love Your Pets

Sung to: *"Row, Row, Row Your Boat"*

Love, love, love your pets
Every single day.
Give them food and water, too.
Then let them run and play.

Elizabeth McKinnon

I Love Mommy

Sung to: *"Frere Jacques"*

I love Mommy, I love Mommy,
Yes, I do, yes, I do.
Mommies are for hugging,
(*Hug self.*)
Mommies are for kissing.
(*Blow a kiss.*)
I love you, yes, I do.
(*Point to mother.*)

Barbara Fletcher

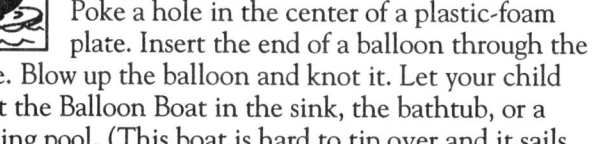
"Shapely" Necklace

Cut 3-inch circles, squares, and triangles from assorted colors of tissue paper. Poke a hole in the center of each shape. Cut a drinking straw into short sections. Help your child string the shapes and straw sections onto pieces of yarn about 2 feet in length. (Make sure that one end of the yarn has been knotted.) When finished, tie the ends of one of the pieces of yarn in a knot and let your child slip the necklace over his or her head.

Water Writer

Rinse out a liquid dishwashing detergent bottle and fill it with water. Show your child how to squeeze water out of the bottle to make designs on a cement patio, a sidewalk, or a wooden deck. Then watch the designs disappear as the water evaporates.

Dandelion-Seed Picture

Take your child outside to find dandelions that have gone to seed. Let your child brush glue all over a piece of dark-colored construction paper. Then help your child hold the paper behind some dandelions while you both blow the seeds onto the paper. Talk about the color of dandelions before and after they have gone to seed.

Through the Forest

You and your child can pretend to be different forest animals. Can you fly like birds, scamper like chipmunks, leap gracefully like deer, lumber along like bears, and be sly like foxes?

Writing and Rolling

Pry the roller ball off an empty roll-on deodorant bottle. Wash the ball and bottle thoroughly and allow them to dry. Fill the bottle with thin tempera paint and replace the roller top. Your child can use the roll-on bottle to draw lines, shapes, or letters on sheets of paper.

On-the-Go Game

While traveling in the car, choose a category such as animals. Your family can take turns naming as many different kinds of animals as they can. Take turns choosing categories (foods, toys, things found in the house, etc.).

Balloon Boat

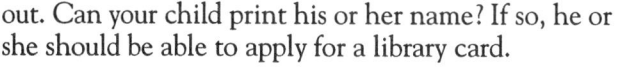

Poke a hole in the center of a plastic-foam plate. Insert the end of a balloon through the hole. Blow up the balloon and knot it. Let your child float the Balloon Boat in the sink, the bathtub, or a wading pool. (This boat is hard to tip over and it sails well in a breeze.)

Library Visit

Take your child to the library and let him or her choose a book or a cassette tape to check out. Can your child print his or her name? If so, he or she should be able to apply for a library card.

Paddle Walk

Give your child a large spatula and a foam-rubber ball. Have your child balance the ball on the spatula as he or she walks in a straight line. As your child's skill increases, have him or her walk in a zigzag line or up and down steps.

Smart Shopping

Give your child a limited selection of coupons and let him or her select two or three favorite foods. Then go to the grocery store and help your child find the coupon items on the shelves. Then let him or her help you prepare or serve these foods at mealtime or for a snack.

Yarn-Ball Catch

Wrap yarn around a 3-inch width of cardboard 25 times. Slide the cardboard out and tie the yarn together in the middle with a 2-foot length of yarn. Clip the looped ends of the yarn and fluff them into a ball. Make a scoop by cutting the bottom off of a bleach bottle at an angle. Use yarn to tie the ball to the handle of the scoop. Take turns with your child tossing up and catching the yarn ball with the scoop.

Happy Book

Discuss with your child the kinds of things that make him or her happy. Help your child draw each of these things on separate sheets of paper. Ask your child to dictate a short description for you to write at the top or bottom of each page. Punch holes on the left-hand side of the sheets and fasten with metal rings or loops of yarn.

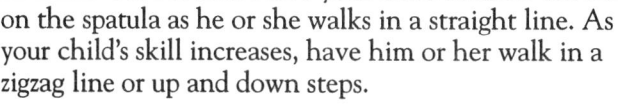

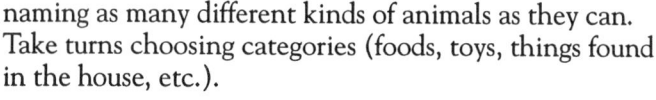

When Friends Visit
Shadow Tag

Take your child and his or her friends outside on a sunny day. Choose a child to be It. Have It try to step on another child's shadow. When It steps on someone's shadow, that child becomes the next It.

Special Day Celebration
National Dairy Month

June has been designated as the time to say "thank you" to cows for all the dairy products we enjoy. Talk with your child about cows (where they live, how they are milked, etc.). How many different kinds of dairy products can you name? Make some butter (see directions at right). If possible, drive to a farm and visit the cows.

Making Butter

Fill a baby-food jar half full of whipping cream. Screw the lid on tightly. Take turns with your child shaking the jar. After about six minutes, the cream will be whipped. After another minute or so, lumps of yellow butter will form. Rinse off the liquid whey and add a little salt for taste before spreading the butter on crackers.

Thank You, Dad

Sung to: *"Jingle Bells"*

Thank you, Dad,
Thank you, Dad,
Thanks for loving me.
Hugs and kisses, hugs and kisses
Come to you from me!

Thank you, Dad,
Thank you, Dad,
You are such a friend.
On this day I'd like to say
On you I can depend!

Becky Valenick

Listening

Young children learn a great deal about the world around them through listening. They listen to different sounds and must rely on their listening skills for following directions at home and in school. You can help your 5-year-old become a good listener by encouraging your youngster to:

- play listening games such as "Simon Says" or "Red Rover."
- listen to songs, stories, riddles, and rhymes.
- identify sounds made by animals and objects found in the home and outdoors.
- follow a sequence of three instructions. (For example: "Put on your sweater, wash your hands, and turn off the light.")
- repeat a nonsense sentence. (For example: "I saw a green cat driving a truck!")
- march to music.
- play musical instruments while listening to music.

Totline® Fun   ●   **Just for Five's**

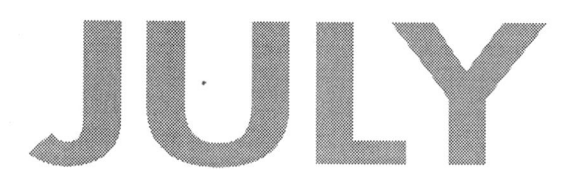

Totline® Fun For JULY

Stars-and-Stripes Collage

Cut several 1-by-9-inch stripes out of red and white construction paper. Help your child glue the stripes onto a sheet of blue construction paper. Add silver star stickers to create a stars-and-stripes design.

Measuring Shadows

On a sunny day, stand a small potted tree (or other appropriate object) on a cement surface. Each hour, use a different-colored piece of chalk to outline the tree's shadow. Then help your child measure and compare the different shadow lengths.

Add-a-Stroke

On separate sheets of paper, draw simple geometric shapes (squares, diamonds, circles, etc.), leaving off one side of each shape. Show your child how to complete the shapes by drawing lines with crayons or felt-tip markers.

Ant Patrol

Take your child on a search for ants to observe them in their natural habitat. Ants tend to make nests under boards, rocks, or leaves. If you can't go to the ants, try making them come to you by placing a small bit of fruit outside as bait. Return to the fruit an hour later to watch the ants that have found it. Observe how they work together to carry it to their nest.

Blueberry Juice Art

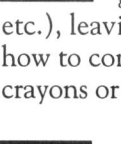

Drain the juice from a package of frozen blueberries into a small bowl. Join your child in using the juice to paint designs on white construction paper or paper towels. (Be careful of juice stains on clothing.) Point out that the skins of the blueberries are blue, yet the juice is more of a purple color. (Use the drained blueberries to make muffins.)

My Telephone Book

Teach your child how to dial 911 (or 0) and the telephone numbers of relatives or friends who could help in an emergency. Write the numbers on separate index cards. Glue photos of these individuals on their corresponding telephone cards. Then fasten them together with small metal rings to make a telephone book for your child. Add a card with your child's photo and your telephone number for the book's cover.

Exploring With Ice

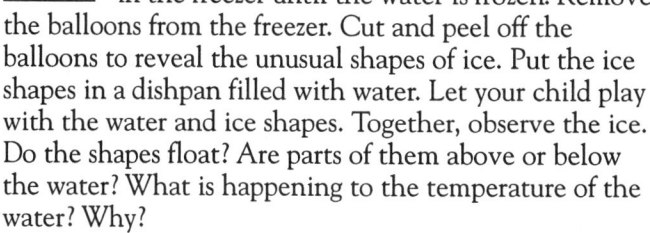

Partially fill balloons with water. Place them in the freezer until the water is frozen. Remove the balloons from the freezer. Cut and peel off the balloons to reveal the unusual shapes of ice. Put the ice shapes in a dishpan filled with water. Let your child play with the water and ice shapes. Together, observe the ice. Do the shapes float? Are parts of them above or below the water? What is happening to the temperature of the water? Why?

Homemade Sand Scoop

Make a sand scoop by cutting off (at an angle) the bottom end of a plastic gallon bottle, leaving the handle intact on the top. (Make sure that the bottle has been thoroughly washed.) Smooth the rough edges with sandpaper. Your child will have fun using this recycled sand tool.

Playing Police Officer

Pretend to be a police officer. Ask your child: "What is your name? Where do you live? What is your telephone number?" Then let your child be the police officer and ask you the questions.

Floor Letters

Make large alphabet letters on the floor with pieces of masking tape. Take turns with your child walking, skipping, and crawling on the letters.

Spaghetti Mobiles

Cook, drain, and cool a small amount of spaghetti. Help your child dip one noodle at a time into containers of glue that have been tinted with different colors of food coloring. Lay the noodles on waxed paper to dry (drying takes 1 or 2 days). Then remove the noodles from the tray and tie a different length of yarn to each noodle. Tie the noodles to a hanger and the mobile is ready to be hung.

Parts of Literature

When reading to your child, ask questions such as "Which part of the book did you like best? Which part made you happy? Which part made you scared? Which part was longest? Which part made you laugh?" Be sure to share your feelings about the book, too!

When Friends Visit
Hiding Game

While playing outside in a sandbox, have the children takes turns closing their eyes while others hide small plastic toys in mounds of sand. Let the children open their eyes and search in the mounds for the toys.

Friends

Sung to: *"Jack and Jill"*

I have a friend, (his/her) name is____,
And we have fun together.
We laugh and play and sing all day
In any kind of weather.

Ruth Miller

Special Day Celebration
National Blueberry Month

Since fresh blueberries are plentiful during midsummer, have some available for your child to taste and examine. Talk about the color and shape of the berries. Help your child discover the little "stars" on the ends. If possible, visit a farm where you can pick your own berries. You can even paint with blueberry juice and make blueberry muffins.

Learning School Lingo

A frustrating hurdle that your child may encounter when he or she first enters school is understanding unfamiliar verbal commands that are seldom explained. To save confusion and misunderstandings, you can anticipate many of the language obstacles and familiarize your preschool child with these commands. Verbal commands can include such phrases as:

in the front	stand still	give me your ears
in the rear	in the back	one at a time
single file	in the middle	behind one another
in a row	all eyes on the board	right-hand corner
in two rows	straight lines	push your chair in
get a partner	clear off your desk	listen carefully
next to	collect the papers	get ready
between	facing me	on top of
alongside	hands to your sides	around the corner
top	pay attention	sit up straight and tall
bottom	all eyes forward	raise your hand
line up	I want your eyes	remain seated

There are many games and activities incorporating these commands that you can play with your child. Games help children learn verbal commands in a relaxed, fun atmosphere rather than in a tense, unsure situation at school. For example, throughout the day challenge your child to understand and follow these directions.

The Ants Go Marching

Sung to: *"When Johnny Comes Marching Home"*

The ants go marching one by one,
Hurrah! Hurrah!
The ants go marching one by one,
Hurrah! Hurrah!
The ants go marching one by one,
Watching ants is lots of fun,
So let's all go marching
One by one by one.

Additional verse: The ants go marching two by two/Worker ants have lots to do.

Adapted Traditional

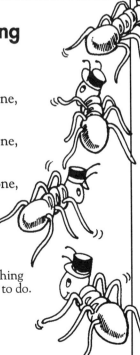

AUGUST

Shape Puzzles

Cut four or five large index cards into two-part puzzles. Draw a different basic shape (circle, triangle, square, rectangle, etc.) on one part of each puzzle and a matching shape on the other part. Mix up the puzzle pieces and have your child find the matching pieces and fit them together.

Bubble Solution

Combine 2 cups liquid dishwashing detergent, 4 cups water, and ½ cup light corn syrup in a jar, a bowl, or a container with a lid. Gently stir the mixture. Let it sit for a few hours before using. (Note: The ground may become slippery where the bubbles pop.)

Bubble-Blower Six-Pack

Fasten pipe-cleaner handles onto the sides of a plastic six-pack holder. Dip it into Bubble Solution (see recipe above). Show your child how to make bubbles by gently swirling the holder through the air.

Reflections of You

Join your child in a search around the room for objects in which you can see your reflections. What do the objects have in common? (They are all smooth and shiny.)

Labels, Labels Everywhere

While shopping at the grocery store, point to various food labels and read some of the words to your child. Point out the signs suspended from the ceiling that identify the aisles.

Art With Reusables

Collect reusable items such as plastic containers and lids, packaging materials, cardboard boxes, fabric and yarn scraps, and paper. Help your child use these materials to create art by using glue, tape, or staples to fasten the reusables together.

Fun With Cardboard Tubes

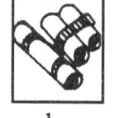

Use cardboard tubes for making telephones or telescopes. Tape two short tubes together to make a pair of binoculars. Or add crepe-paper streamers to the end of a long tube to create a magic wand.

Homemade Building Blocks

Cut the tops off pairs of cardboard milk cartons and discard. To make a block, fit one carton inside the other. Make as many blocks as you wish.

Beach-Blanket Hiding Game

Take turns hiding a familiar object under a beach blanket. Try to guess what it is by looking at its shape and, if necessary, feeling the object through the blanket. You can even give clues. Lift up the blanket to see if your guess was correct.

Sponge Toss

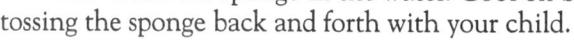

Set out a bucket of water and a large sponge. Soak the sponge in the water. Cool off by tossing the sponge back and forth with your child.

Ice Experiment

Fill a freezer-safe container, such as a gelatin mold, a resealable plastic bag, or a plastic food-storage container, with water. Freeze the water into a solid block of ice. Place the ice in a shallow pan and let your child spoon salt onto the ice. Wherever the salt touches the ice, the ice will melt faster. Soon the ice will be full of holes. Talk about how the ice has changed.

Wormy Apples

Cut five apple shapes out of 5-inch squares of posterboard or heavy paper. Color the apples red. Cut one finger hole in the first shape, two finger holes in the second shape, three holes in the third shape, and so on. Mark each apple with the numeral that matches the number of holes in it. Take turns with your child choosing an apple shape, sticking your fingers through the holes, and naming the number of "worms" you see.

Homemade Stickers

Make a grid of 1-inch squares on a piece of paper. Let your child use a rubber stamp and stamp pad to place an image in each of the squares. Combine 1 packet unflavored gelatin, 6 tablespoons warm water, and ½ teaspoon vanilla or mint flavoring. Use a paintbrush to apply the glue mixture to the back of the sheet of paper. Let the mixture dry. Your child can use the stickers by licking the backs or by moistening them with a damp sponge.

When Friends Visit
Let's Build Together

Set out a box of blocks. Have one child begin by choosing a block from the box and placing it in the middle of the floor. Then have each child take a turn choosing a block and adding it to the first one to create a block sculpture. Continue until all the blocks have been used.

Special Day Celebration
National Aviation Day

August 19 has been chosen to honor Orville and Wilbur Wright, the brothers who made the first airplane flight in 1903 at Kitty Hawk, North Carolina. To celebrate, look through magazines for different kinds of aircraft—jets, propeller planes, helicopters, gliders, and space ships. Take a trip to a local airport and learn the song "I'm an Airplane," below.

I'm an Airplane
Sung to: *"Clementine"*

I'm an airplane, I'm an airplane,
Flying up into the sky.
Flying higher, flying higher,
As I watch the clouds go by.

I'm an airplane, I'm an airplane,
See me flying all around.
Flying lower, flying lower,
Till I land down on the ground.

Pretend to be airplanes and act out the movements as you sing.

Elizabeth McKinnon

Fluffy Treat

Pour ¼ cup water into a bowl. Add 2 envelopes unflavored gelatin. Stir and let sit for 5 minutes. Add ¾ cup boiling water and ¼ teaspoon red food coloring. Stir until gelatin is dissolved. Pour the mixture into a blender container. Add 1 can (6 ounces) unsweetened frozen apple-juice concentrate. Blend until fluffy. Pour into small paper cups. Chill for about 15 minutes.

Starting School

Starting school should be an exciting event for your child. You can help make this a happy experience by doing several things to build your child's enthusiasm and self-confidence. Your child will feel more comfortable when he or she knows what to expect. Before school starts:

- Teach your child the safest route to school. Take your child to the bus stop or walk to school together several times. Point out crosswalks, driveways, and traffic lights. Discuss not talking to strangers.

- Visit the school grounds so that they are familiar to your child.

- Help your child develop a daily routine such as going to bed early and dressing him or herself without help.

- Talk enthusiastically about what school will be like.

- Discuss any fears your child may have about starting school. If you are excited and confident, your child will be, too.

- Make starting school an exciting event by shopping for a special pencil box or lunch box.

♦♦♦ Totline® Fun For
SEPTEMBER

Save a Tree

Explain to your child that recycling a 3-foot stack of newspaper will save one tree from being cut down and turned into paper. Then put a piece of masking tape 3 feet up on a wall in your child's room. Have your child place newspapers in a pile under the tape. Each time a 3-foot stack is collected, take the stack to a recycling center and put a mark on a tree-shaped chart. At the end of the month or other specified time, count how many trees your child has saved. Then celebrate by going outside and having a picnic under a tree.

All Aboard!

Set out two piles of identical small blocks. Ask your child to guess if there is the same number of blocks in each pile. Have your child test his or her guess by lining up the blocks from each pile next to each other to create two "trains." Then count the numbers of blocks in the two trains to see if they match. (Block towers can be made instead of trains.)

Fingerprinting

Explain to your child that each person has a unique fingerprint pattern made of loops, arches, and whorls. Rub a light coating of dark lipstick on the pads of your child's fingertips. Show your child how to make fingerprints by pressing each finger on white paper. Make your fingerprints below these. Use a magnifying glass to compare both sets of prints. Use felt-tip markers to transform the fingerprints into creatures.

Fall Face

Cut a 4 ½-inch-diameter circle out of construction paper. Collect a variety of fall leaves. Help your child glue the circle on a sheet of paper. Then join your child in gluing the leaves around the circle for hair. Add facial features with felt-tip markers.

Game Box

Find a small rubber ball. In the bottom of a facial-tissue box, cut a hole that is slightly larger than the ball. Show your child how to play the game by dropping the ball through the opening on top of the box and moving the box all around to make the ball roll out the hole in the bottom of the box. Take turns playing the game.

Muddy Water

Partially fill a clear jar with dirt and water. Stir the mixture. Observe what happens. Continue to watch the jar and discuss the changes that are occurring. Why is the dirt sinking to the bottom? What would happen if you stirred it up again?

Invisible Ink

Let your child paint with lemon juice on white paper. Let the pictures dry and then press a hot iron over them to bring out the Invisible Ink.

Playdough Moons

Let your child form "moons" out of balls of white playdough by making holes for craters and pinching the dough to make ridges.

Moonbeam Game

Have your family sit on the floor in a circle. Choose someone to be the Moon, who will stand in the middle of the circle and hold a flashlight. Let the Moon close his or her eyes, slowly turn in a circle, open his or her eyes, and shine the flashlight moonbeam on the first person he or she sees. That person will become the new Moon. Let everyone have a turn.

Stop and Listen

Take your child on a walk through a park or the woods. Walk slowly and stop frequently to look carefully around. Ask your child what he or she sees. Have your child close his or her eyes and listen to the sounds. What is making those sounds? Have your child stand quietly in one place and look for birds or squirrels.

Bouncing Ball

Give your child a ball that bounces well. Show him or her how to bounce the ball against a wall. Have your child try to catch the ball after it bounces one, two, or three times.

For the Birds

Give your child an empty toilet-tissue tube. Help your child spread peanut butter all over the outside of the tube and then roll it in birdseed. Take your child outside and show him or her how to place the feeder over small, vertical twigs on the branches of trees.

When Friends Visit
Stop-and-Go Game

Have the children dance or move to music. Everyone must stop when you say "stop." Let the children begin moving again when you say "go." Take turns being the person to say "stop" or "go."

Special Day Celebration
Pickle Day

The pickle, the world's most humorous vegetable, is officially recognized during "Snack-a-Pickle Time," which falls on the last 10 days of September. During this time, pay tribute to pickles by preparing pickle snacks, comparing their tastes and sizes, and reciting the tongue twister "Peter Piper Picked a Peck of Pickled Peppers" (at right.)

Sleeping Pickle

Spread one side of a bread slice with margarine. Place it buttered side up on an ungreased baking sheet. Top bread with a slice of lunchmeat. Place half of a pickle on the slice of meat. Cover pickle with a cheese-slice "blanket," leaving the top portion of pickle exposed. Bake at 400°F for 7 to 8 minutes or until edges of bread are crisp and cheese is melted.

Peter Piper Picked a Peck of Pickled Peppers

Recite this tongue twister and let your child have fun trying to repeat it after you.

Peter Piper picked a peck of pickled peppers,
A peck of pickled peppers Peter Piper picked.
If Peter Piper picked a peck of pickled peppers,
Where's the peck of pickled peppers Peter Piper
   picked?

Traditional

Falling Leaves

Sung to: *"Hickory, Dickory, Dock"*

Little leaves falling down,
Red, yellow, orange, and brown.
   (Flutter fingers downward.)
Whirling, twirling round and round,
Falling to the ground.
   (Flutter fingers downward in circles.)

Adapted Traditional

A Great Start

When school begins, start your child off right each day by making sure he or she:

- is well rested.
- is well nourished.
- has enough time to get ready for school.
- wears comfortable clothes.

Show interest in your child by listening to what he or she has to say about school. Praise your child for the work that he or she has done. Show support and enthusiasm for your child by staying in touch with the teacher, joining the school's PTA, attending parent programs and conferences, and volunteering to help with class projects.

Totline® Fun

Just for Five's

✳✳✳ Totline® Fun For

OCTOBER

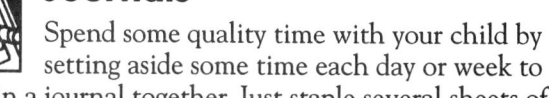

Clipping Tubes

Cut cardboard tubes into 2-inch lengths. Have your child use spring-type clothespins to clip the tubes together to make simple designs. You can also ask your child to clip specific numbers of tubes together.

Torn-Paper Pumpkin

Give your child a small paper plate and a piece of orange construction paper. Let your child tear the orange paper into small pieces and glue the pieces all over the paper plate. Then let your child glue on a green construction-paper stem to complete the pumpkin.

Ghostly Family

On a sheet of white paper, help your child trace around your family's hands. Cut out the shapes. Have your child turn the hand shapes into ghosts by turning the hand shapes upside down and using black crayons to draw eyes on the palms of the hands. Glue the ghosts onto a large sheet of black construction paper so that they appear to be floating in the night sky. Which ghost is the smallest? the largest?

Trick-or-Treat Container

Cut the top off a plastic gallon milk jug, leaving the handle attached to the bottom. Cut out shapes from construction paper and help your child glue them onto the jug to create a funny or scary face. Glue pieces of yarn around the top edge of the jug for hair.

News for Everyone

Share the newspaper with your child. Read the comics and the captions under interesting pictures. Point to letters that are in your child's name. Look for numerals in the advertisement pages.

Measuring a Pumpkin

Set out a pumpkin. Let your child cut off a length of yarn that he or she thinks will fit around the pumpkin. Have your child try wrapping the yarn around the pumpkin to see how well it fits. Measure and cut off a piece of yarn that fits around the pumpkin exactly. Let your child compare his or her yarn piece to the one that fits. Ask, "Is your yarn piece shorter or longer?"

Journals

Spend some quality time with your child by setting aside some time each day or week to write in a journal together. Just staple several sheets of paper together to make a journal and have your child dictate something for you to write. Try offering a topic each time such as "What did you do last night? What makes you happy? What is your favorite game?"

What Is Litter?

Set out various pieces of litter (soda can, gum wrapper, plastic bag, paper, etc.) and nature objects (leaf, branch, rock, etc.). Ask your child to point to the objects that are litter. How does your child know that the objects are litter? What should be done with them? Hide some litter around the room, and let your child search for it and put it in a garbage bag.

Marble Fun

Tie several marbles in the toe of a large sock. Have your child feel the sock and try to guess how many marbles are inside. Take out the marbles and count them. Take turns placing marbles in the sock and guessing.

Jack-O'-Lantern Flashlight

From orange construction paper, cut a circle to cover the end of a flashlight. Cut jack-o'-lantern features out of the circle. Tape the circle to the end of the flashlight. Darken the room, play music, and let your child use the flashlight to shine jack-o'-lanterns on everything while dancing around the room.

Tennis-Ball Carry

Place a large spoon and a basket filled with tennis balls at one end of the room and an empty basket at the other end. Let your child balance a tennis ball on the spoon, walking carefully across the room, and put the ball in the other basket.

Sniffy Name

Place a sheet of construction paper inside a box lid. Help your child print his or her name by squeezing glue onto the paper. Then let your child sprinkle fruit-flavored gelatin powder on the glue and tap the excess into the box lid. After the glue dries, let your child let everyone sniff his or her name.

When Friends Visit
Flavored Popcorn

Let your child and his or her friends help you make popcorn. Place some of the popcorn in three plastic sandwich bags or three paper lunch sacks. Add a pinch of Parmesan cheese, taco seasoning, or a mixture of cinnamon and sugar to each bag. Let the children shake the bags to distribute the seasonings. Taste the popcorn from each bag and discuss the flavors. Which flavors do the children like best?

Special Day Celebration
National Popcorn Month

Popcorn has had a long history in our country. Native Americans used it for food as well as for decorations in necklaces and headdresses. At the first Thanksgiving, they introduced popcorn to the Pilgrims. Have fun preparing and eating flavored popcorn (recipe above). Can your child guess what makes popcorn pop? Inside each kernel is a tiny pocket of water. When the water becomes hot, it expands so much that it bursts open the hard outer shell.

Orange Lemonade Experiment

Use water tinted with red food coloring to make partially frozen ice cubes. Pour a glass of yellow lemonade and ask your child what might happen if you add a red ice cube to the lemonade. Place a red ice cube in the lemonade and have your child stir the lemonade and observe the color change.

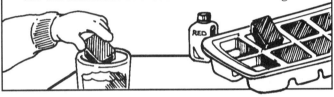

Taking the Scare Out of Halloween

Halloween time can be overwhelming for young children. Decorations are displayed weeks before the holiday, confusing children who have little concept of time. Scary costumes and spooky noises can frighten youngsters who have difficulty distinguishing between real and make-believe. The following are a few ideas to help make Halloween a non-threatening, safe time for your child.

- Instead of having a costume party, have a pajama party. Have the guests wear their favorite pajamas to the party and bring their favorite dolls or stuffed animals.

- Provide a comfortable way for your child to talk about the things that scare him or her. Let him or her know that everybody is frightened sometimes.

- If you opt to have a Halloween celebration, remember that commercial sound effects may be too intense for young children. Instead, let your child and friends or family make tape recordings of "spooky" Halloween sounds.

Halloween Is Here

Sung to: *"The Farmer in the Dell"*

Oh, Halloween is here,
Oh, Halloween is here.
Heigh-ho, the derry-oh.
Oh, Halloween is here.

We'll all give a cheer,
We'll all give a cheer.
Heigh-ho, the derry-oh.
Oh, Halloween is here.

Judith McNitt

 **Totline® Fun For**

NOVEMBER

Family Reading Time

Set aside 10 or 15 minutes each evening for the entire family to relax and read books, magazines, or newspapers. Make sure the television is off.

Feathers or Fur?

Explain to your child that birds have feathers on the outer parts of their bodies, while other animals have fur. Find pictures of birds and other animals in magazines and cut them out. Hold up each picture and ask your child to tell you if feathers or fur cover the animal. What do the animals covered with feathers have in common?

Fun With Brown

Glue scraps of wood together to make sculptures. Make gingerbread. Use cardboard cartons for stacking and building. Fingerpaint brown designs on a brown paper sack, or print with potato halves and brown tempera paint.

Frontier Vest

Cut a neck hole in the bottom of a large brown paper bag. Cut out two arm holes in the sides of the bag. Cut open the front of the bag from the top edge up to the neck hole. Use crayons and felt-tip markers to help your child decorate the vest. Cut fringes around the lower edges of the vest.

What Am I Wearing?

Wrap a blanket around yourself. Ask your child to describe the clothes that you are wearing. This game helps sharpen your child's ability to make observations. Invite family members to join in the fun.

Circle Family

Cut circles of different sizes from various colors of construction paper. Help your child glue an appropriate-size circle to represent each family member on a sheet of white construction paper. Use crayons or felt-tip markers to add arms, legs, facial features, and other details. (Glue on small paper triangles to represent pets.) Write "My Family" at the top of the paper and the appropriate family member's name next to each circle. Hang up the paper for everyone to admire!

Thanksgiving Dinner

Make several batches of colored playdough. For each batch, combine 1 cup flour, 1/2 cup salt, 6 to 7 tablespoons water, 1 tablespoon vegetable oil, and several drops food coloring. Help your child use a rolling pin, cookie cutters, and other kitchen gadgets to create "Thanksgiving Day foods" with the playdough. Arrange the foods on a paper plate.

Thankful Hands

Ask your child to think of five things for which he or she is thankful. Then help your child trace around his or her hand on construction paper and cut out the shape. Write five things your child has said he or she is thankful for on the shape, one on each finger. Let your child decorate the hand shape so that it looks like a turkey.

Corny Napkin Rings

Cut four 2 1/2-inch-long rings out of cardboard tubes. Cut out strips of construction paper to fit around the rings. Glue the strips to the rings and allow them to dry. Then let your child brush glue all over the construction paper and roll the rings in a small plate of popcorn kernels until they are covered.

Doctor's-Office Playtime

Take turns with your child being a doctor, a nurse, and a patient. Take pulses, give pretend shots, listen to hearts, bandage arms and legs, write pretend prescriptions, and give advice to maintain good health such as "Get lots of rest. Drink plenty of fluids. Exercise every day."

How Many Seeds?

Show your child an apple and ask him or her to predict the number of seeds that will be found inside the apple. Cut the apple open crosswise and count the seeds. Compare the number of seeds with your child's prediction.

Feather Dusting

Hand your child a feather duster and give him or her directions to follow such as "Dust under the chair. Dust behind the chair. Dust the back of the chair. Dust the legs of the chair." Now let your child give the directions as you do the dusting.

When Friends Visit
The Bear Bounce

Place a small blanket on the floor. Set a teddy bear in the middle of the blanket. Have each child grab a corner of the blanket. Show the children how to toss and catch the bear with the blanket.

Deviled-Egg Ships

Peel hard-boiled eggs and cut them in half lengthwise. Remove the yolks. Have your child mash the yolks in a bowl with mayonnaise and a small amount of prepared mustard. Spoon the yolk mixture back into the egg-white halves. Make a sail for each ship by poking two holes in a small square of paper and sticking a toothpick in one hole and out the other. Insert a toothpick sail in each Deviled-Egg Ship.

Making Bread
Sung to: "*Frere Jacques*"

Making bread, making bread,
Ummm, good. Ummm, good.
I can smell it baking,
I can smell it baking.
Smells so good, smells so good!

Making bread, making bread,
Ummm, good. Ummm, good.
Now it's time for tasting,
Now it's time for tasting.
Tastes so good, tastes so good!

Elizabeth McKinnon

Thanksgiving Time
Sung to: "*The Farmer in the Dell*"

Thanksgiving time is here.
Let's give a great big cheer
For food and friends and family.
Thanksgiving time is here.

Gayle Bittinger

Special Day Celebration
National Children's Book Week

Plan to visit the public library during this event, which is celebrated the third week in November. Many libraries have special displays and programs that invite children to explore the wonderful world of books. Don't forget to read to your child at bedtime!

Cooking With Your Child

When choosing a recipe to prepare with your child, look for one that offers lots of opportunities for chopping, measuring, sifting, mixing, pouring, and mashing. Avoid recipes where most of the preparation is done on the stovetop. Involve your child from beginning to end. The day before a cooking activity, let him or her help you develop a shopping list. On cooking day, let him or her help set up by setting out unbreakable bowls, pans, and utensils. Provide your child with safe, child-size utensils for chopping, stirring, and mixing. Your child's involvement needn't end when the recipe goes into the oven. Let him or her help set and clear the table, wash and dry dishes and tabletops, sweep floors, and put things away. Have a fun and educational cooking experience.

DECEMBER

Seasonal Paper Chains

Help your child tape together 1-by-8-inch strips of construction paper to create a chain that contains as many loops as there are days remaining before a holiday or a special event. Let your child count the loops each time one is added to the chain. Each day, have your child remove one of the loops and count the remaining loops to determine how many days are left before the holiday.

Christmas Concentration

Cut out matching pairs of small pictures from holiday wrapping paper. Glue each picture on an index card. To play, spread the cards face down on the floor. Take turns turning up two cards. If the pictures match, keep the cards. If the pictures don't match, replace them face down in their same positions on the floor. Continue playing until all the cards have been matched. Who has earned the most cards?

Button Christmas Tree

Cut a Christmas tree shape out of green construction paper. Set out glue and an assortment of buttons. Have your child dip the buttons into the glue and place them all over the Christmas-tree shape. If desired, use a loop of yarn to hang the button ornament on your tree.

Letters, Letters Everywhere

Whenever your child expresses interest in a letter from the alphabet, help him or her discover that letter on book covers, cereal boxes, soup cans, or pages from the newspaper. Take your child for a walk in the neighborhood and look for that letter on street signs and billboards.

Holiday Storytime

Have your child "read" his or her favorite holiday story to you or other family members or friends. Your child will also enjoy reading the story to his or her favorite toys.

Recycled Cards

Provide your child with bits of wrapping paper, ribbons, and pictures cut from leftover greeting cards. Let him or her glue these materials to heavy paper to make unique homemade cards.

Recipe-Card Holder

Help your child cover a cardboard toilet-tissue tube with a piece of self-stick paper or a piece of wallpaper and glue. Cut two 1-inch slits (directly opposite each other) in the top end of the tube. On an index card write the following message: "Please think of me when you use a recipe. Love, (your child's name)." Insert the card into the slits at the top of the decorated tube. Give as a gift to someone special.

Dreidel Painting

Collect a dreidel or a top. Set out the dreidel along with a sheet of white construction paper and a shallow container of blue tempera paint. Let your child practice spinning the dreidel on a flat surface with his or her fingers. Then let him or her dip the end of the dreidel into the paint and spin it on the paper to create swirling designs.

Candle Comparisons

Set out five or six candles of various sizes. Have your child use them for the following games: lining up the candles from shortest to tallest; grouping the candles by color; sniffing the candles and trying to identify their scents.

Cinnamon-Dough Decorations

To make cinnamon dough, in a bowl mix together four parts cinnamon, three parts applesauce, and one part glue. Help your child flatten the dough on a floured surface and use cookie cutters to cut shapes from the dough. Use a straw to cut a hole in the top of each shape so it can be hung after drying for at least 48 hours.

String Shapes

Cut two pieces of string or yarn into 3-foot lengths. Tell your child, "Let's each make a circle on the floor with our pieces of string; Let's stand inside our circles...jump out of our circles, etc. Let's turn our circles into triangles...into lines, etc."

Me and My Shadow

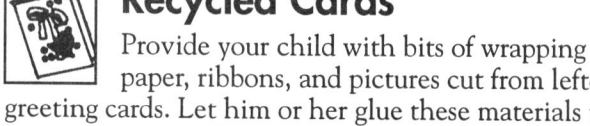

Shine light from a lamp or a flashlight onto a bare wall. Turn off the other lights in the room. Show your child how to stand in front of the bright light and experiment with making shadows. Make big shadows, little shadows, animal shadows, dancing shadows, etc.

When Friends Visit
Handy Wreath

Help your child and his or her friends trace around their hands on red and green construction paper. Help them cut out the hand shapes. Overlap and attach the hand shapes in a circle on a large piece of butcher paper to make a wreath. Then cut a large bow out of red construction paper and glue it to the bottom of the wreath.

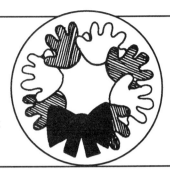

Yule-Log Sandwiches

Help your child flatten slices of wheat bread with a rolling pin, spread softened cream cheese on each slice, and sprinkle on diced red and green bell pepper slices. Then let your child roll up the bread slices to make "yule logs." (You can use peanut butter and jam instead of cream cheese and peppers.)

Relaxing Fun

Provide your child with plenty of tension-reducing, tactile experiences this holiday season. Fill plastic dishpans or large plastic containers with warm, soapy water.

Special Day Celebration
Poinsettia Day

December 12 is the day for enjoying poinsettias and for remembering Dr. Joel R. Poinsett, the man who introduced the native Mexican plant in the United States and for whom the poinsettia is named. Take your child to the supermarket to see poinsettias on display.

Five Little Bells

Five little bells hanging in a row,
   (Hold up five fingers.)
The first bell said, "Ring me slow."
   (Point to thumb.)
The second bell said, "Ring me fast,"
   (Point to index finger.)
The third bell said, "Ring me last."
   (Point to middle finger.)
The fourth bell said, "I'm like a chime,"
   (Point to ring finger.)
The fifth bell said, "It's Christmas time."
   (Bend little finger up and down.)

Adapted Traditional

Spin the Dreidel

Sung to: *"Twinkle, Twinkle, Little Star"*

Spin the dreidel round and round,
It spins fast and then falls down.
It starts out fast and then spins slow,
Wobble, wobble, down it goes.
Spin the dreidel round and round,
It spins fast and then falls down.

Judy Caplan Ginsburgh

Toys

Toys are important learning tools for children. They help expand your child's abilities to concentrate, solve problems, and be creative. Toys are also useful for developing eye-hand coordination and strengthening your child's body muscles. You may find that some of your child's favorite toys are those made from items found in your home. In any case, be sure that the toys your child uses are safe.

- Balls
- Beanbags
- Bicycle
- Blocks (all sizes)
- Books
- Bowling set
- Camera
- Card and board games (simple ones)
- Cash register and play money
- Clay
- Climbing equipment (jungle gym, seesaw, etc.)
- Computer
- Cooking equipment
- Crafts (loop looms, etc.)
- Crayons
- Doctor kit
- Dollhouse with furniture
- Drawing materials
- Dress-up clothes
- Fingerpaints
- Flashlight
- Housekeeping equipment

- Jump rope
- Kite
- Magnetic letters and numerals
- Miniature people, animals, farms, vehicles, etc.
- Musical instruments
- Paints and paintbrushes
- Picture lacing cards
- Plastic bat and balls
- Puppets
- Puzzles
- Roller skates
- Science materials (magnets, magnifying glass, etc.)
- Scooter
- Stencils
- Tape recorder and tapes
- Toy clock
- Trains
- Typewriter
- Wagon
- Wheel toys (trucks, farm vehicles, etc.)
- Workbench (with real child-size tools)

Toy Safety
Your child's toys should:
- be well made and durable.
- be finished with non-toxic materials.
- not have parts that can pinch fingers.
- not have long cords that could accidentally strangle.
- not have sharp points or edges.

Books for 5-Year-Olds

This is only a partial list. Check the library for other books your 5-year-old will enjoy.

The Bear and the Mountain, Jean Warren, Illus. by Judy Shimono. Warren Publishing House, 1994.

A Birthday for Frances, Russell Hoban, Illus. by Lillian Hoban. Harper & Row, 1968.

Chicka Chicka Boom Boom, Bill Martin Jr. and John Archambault, Illus. by Lois Ehlert. Simon & Schuster, 1989.

Daddies at Work, Eve Merriam, Illus. by Eugenie Fernandes. Simon & Schuster, 1989.

Dandelion, Don Freeman. Puffin Books, 1964.

Ellie the Evergreen, Jean Warren, Illus. by Gwen Connelly. Warren Publishing House, 1993.

Happy Birthday, Moon, Frank Asch. Simon & Schuster, 1989.

Huff and Puff Seasonal Adventure Series, Jean Warren, Illus. by Molly Piper. Warren Publishing House, 1993–1995.

Ira Sleeps Over, Bernard Waber. Houghton Mifflin, 1972.

Joey, Jack Kent. Simon & Schuster, 1984.

Katy and the Big Snow, Virginia Lee Burton. Houghton Mifflin, 1943.

Keep Your Mouth Closed Dear, Aliki. Dial Press, 1966.

Leo the Late Bloomer, Robert Kraus. Simon & Schuster, 1987.

Little Rabbit's Loose Tooth, Lucy Bate, Illus. by Diane Degroat. Crown Publishers, 1975.

Lovable Lyle, Bernard Waber. Houghton Mifflin, 1969.

Mike Mulligan and His Steam Shovel, Virginia Lee Burton. Houghton Mifflin, 1939.

Mommies at Work, Eve Merriam, Illus. by Eugenie Fernandes. Simon & Schuster 1989.

Please and Thank You Book, Richard Scarry. Random House, 1973.

The Spooky Old Tree, Stan and Jan Berenstain. Random House, 1978.

Strega Nona, Tomie De Paola. Simon & Schuster, 1975.

The Tale of Peter Rabbit, Beatrix Potter, Illus. by Amye Rosenberg. Western Publishing, 1982.

Those Mean Nasty Dirty Downright Disgusting But…Invisible Germs, Judith Rice, Illus. by Reed Merrill. Redleaf Press, 1989.

The Tiny Seed, Eric Carle. Simon & Schuster, 1987.

Too Much Noise, Ann McGovern, Illus. by Simms Taback. Scholastic, 1967.

Where the Wild Things Are, Maurice Sendak. Harper & Row, 1963.

The Wishing Fish, Jean Warren, Illus. by Barb Tourtillotte. Warren Publishing House, 1993.

Would You Rather Be a Bullfrog?, Theo LeSieg, Illus. by Roy McKie. Random House, 1975.

Books For Parents

Are You Sad Too?: Helping Children Deal With Loss and Death, Dinah Seibert, Judy Drolet, and Joyce V. Fetro. ETR Associates, 1993.

The Art of Sensitive Parenting: The 10 Master Keys to Raising Confident, Competent, and Responsible Children, Katherine C. Kersey. Acropolis Books, 1986.

The Difficult Child, Stanley Turecki. Bantam Publishers, 1989.

Helping Children Cope With Divorce, Edward Teyber. MacMillan, 1994.

The Hurried Child, David Elkind. Addison Wesley Publishers, 1989.

I Want It: A Children's Problem Solving Book, Elizabeth Crary, Illus. by Marina Megale. Parenting Press, 1982.

More Piggyback Songs, Jean Warren, Illus. by Marion Hopping Ekberg. Warren Publishing House, 1984.

The New Read-Aloud Handbook, Jim Trelease. Penguin Books, 1989.

1•2•3 Math: Pre-Math Activities for Young Children, Jean Warren, Illus. by Marion Hopping Ekberg. Warren Publishing House, 1992.

1•2•3 Reading and Writing: Pre-Reading and Pre-Writing Opportunities for Young Children, Jean Warren, Illus. by Marion Hopping Ekberg. Warren Publishing House, 1992.

1•2•3 Science: Science Activities for Young Children, Gayle Bittinger, Illus. by Marion Hopping Ekberg. Warren Publishing House, 1993.

Raising Your Spirited Child, Mary Sheedy Kurcinka. Harper & Row, 1992.

Super Snacks, Jean Warren, Illus. by Glen Mulvey. Warren Publishing House, 1992.

Teaching Children About Food, Christine Berman and Jacki Fromer. Bull Publishing, 1991.

Your Five Year Old (Sunny & Serene), Louise Ames and Frances Ilg. Dell Publishing, 1983.

TOTLINE® books & resources

1•2•3 SERIES

All books in this series present simple, hands-on activities that reflect Totline's commitment to providing open-ended, age-appropriate, cooperative, and no-lose experiences for working with preschool children.

1•2•3 Art
Open-Ended Art
More than 160 pages of art activities emphasize the creative process. All 238 activities use inexpensive, readily available materials. 160 pp.
ISBN 0-911019-06-5 • WPH 0401

1•2•3 Games
Cooperative, No-Lose
Foster creativity and decision-making with 70 no-lose games that are appropriate for a variety of young ages. 80 pp.
ISBN 0-911019-09-X • WPH 0402

1•2•3 Colors
Hundreds of activities for Color Days, including ideas for art, learning games, language, science, movement, music, and snacks. 160 pp.
ISBN 0-911019-17-0 • WPH 0403

1•2•3 Puppets
More than 50 simple puppets to make, including Talking Turkey, Alligator Egg Carton, Willie Worm, Dancing Spoon, and more. 80 pp.
ISBN 0-911019-21-9 • WPH 0404

1•2•3 Books
More than 20 simple beginning-concept books to make, including sequences, stickers, textures, numbers, and weather. 80 pp.
ISBN 0-911019-23-5 • WPH 0406

1•2•3 Reading & Writing
Help young children develop pre-reading and pre-writing skills with more than 250 meaningful and non-threatening activities. 160 pp.
ISBN 0-911019-47-2 • WPH 0407

1•2•3 Rhymes, Stories & Songs
Open-Ended Language
Open-ended rhymes, stories, and songs to capture the interest of young children. 80 pp.
ISBN 0-911019-50-2 • WPH 0408

1•2•3 Math
Non-threatening, hands-on activities, such as counting, sequencing, and sorting, help children develop pre-math skills. 160 pp.
ISBN 0-911019-52-9 • WPH 0409

1•2•3 Science
Help young children develop science skills—observing, estimating, predicting, and more—using ordinary household objects. 160 pp.
ISBN 0-911019-62-6 • WPH 0410

1•2•3 Shapes
Hundreds of activities for exploring the concept of shapes—circles, squares, triangles, rectangles, ovals, diamonds, hearts, and stars. 160 pp.
ISBN 1-57029-006-7 • WPH 0411

CUT & TELL CUTOUTS

These full-color, inexpensive folder stories contain a traditional nursery tale or rhyme retold by Jean Warren. Beautifully illustrated cutouts are ready to turn into flannelboard and magnet board props or stick puppets. Also includes songs, poems, and learning games. Each 8 pp.

NURSERY TALES
• The Gingerbread Kid
• Henny Penny
• The Three Bears
• The Three Billy Goats Gruff
• Little Red Riding Hood
• The Three Little Pigs

MORE NURSERY TALES
• The Big, Big Carrot
• Country Mouse & City Mouse
• The Elves and the Shoemaker
• The Hare and the Tortoise
• The Little Red Hen
• Stone Soup

NUMBER RHYMES
• Hickory, Dickory Dock
• Humpty Dumpty
• 1, 2, Buckle My Shoe
• Old Mother Hubbard
• Rabbit, Rabbit, Carrot Eater
• Twinkle, Twinkle, Little Star

STORY BOOKS WITH ACTIVITIES

Totline story books with activities are written by Jean Warren and illustrated with full-color drawings that are antibias and culturally diverse. Each story is followed by 16 pages of related songs and activities that extend learning—and fun. The Nature series focuses on animals, changes, and differences in nature.

Ellie the Evergreen
Themes: Fall, Winter, Self-esteem
When the trees in the park turn beautiful colors in the fall, Ellie the Evergreen feels left out, until something special happens to her. 32 pp.
ISBN 0-911019067-7 • WPH 1901 • PB

The Wishing Fish
Themes: Trees, North/South, Hot/Cold
A palm tree and a fir tree each gets its wish to move to a different climate—thanks to the magical powers of the rainbow Wishing Fish. 32 pp.
ISBN 0-911019-74-X • WPH 1903 • PB

The Bear and the Mountain
Themes: Bears, Flowers, Friendship
Experience the joy and caring of friendship as a playful bear cub and a lonely mountain get to know each other through the seasons of the year. 32 pp.
ISBN 0-911019-98-7 • WPH 1905 • PB

Ask about Totline's second set of story books—the Huff and Puff series—which features the monthly adventures of two childlike clouds.

BUSY BEES SERIES

For use with two- and three-year-olds. Day-by-day, hands-on projects and movement games are just right for busy hands and feet!

Busy Bees–SPRING
With a focus on spring, more than 60 age-appropriate activities enhance the learning process for busy minds and bodies. 136 pp.
ISBN 1-57029-026-1 • WPH 2407

Busy Bees–SUMMER
It's possible to merge play and learning with the summer edition of Totline's Busy Bees series. 136 pp.
ISBN 1-57029-066-0 • WPH 2408

Busy Bees–FALL
Attention-getting activities with a focus on fall fun! Includes simple songs, rhymes, snacks, movements, art, and science projects. 136 pp.
ISBN 1-57029-008-3 • WPH 2405

Busy Bees–WINTER
Enchant toddlers through the winter months with a wealth of ideas for learning fun, from movement ideas to hands-on projects. 136 pp.
ISBN 1-57029-023-7 • WPH 2406

SNACK SERIES

This series provides easy, educational recipes for healthful eating and fun learning.

Multicultural Snacks
75 recipes from 38 countries let children get a taste of many cultures. Each chapter features one food and different ways to prepare it. 48 pp.
ISBN 1-57029-025-3 • WPH 1604

Super Snacks
Seasonal recipes for snacks with no sugar, honey, or artificial sweeteners! Nutritional analysis and CACFP information included. 48 pp.
ISBN 0-911019-49-9 • WPH 1601

Healthy Snacks
New recipes for healthy alternatives to junk-food snacks at home and school. Low in fat, sugar, and sodium. Nutritional analysis and CACFP information. 48 pp.
ISBN 0-911019-63-4 • WPH 1602

Teaching Snacks
Use snacktime to promote basic skills and concepts with these healthful recipes that turn eating into learning time. 48 pp.
ISBN 0-911019-82-0 • WPH 1603

PIGGYBACK® SONGS

New songs sung to the tunes of childhood favorites. No music to read! Easy for adults and children. Chorded for guitar or autoharp. Nine books in the series!

Piggyback Songs
A seasonal collection of more than 100 original, easy-to-sing songs for children! 64 pp.
ISBN 0-911019-01-4 • WPH 0201

We wish to thank the following teachers, childcare workers, and parents for contributing many of the ideas in this book: Valerie Bielsker, Olathe, KS; Janice Bodenstedt, Jackson, MI; Karen Brown, Dry Ridge, KY; Tamara Clohessy, Eureka, CA; Sarah Cooper, Arlington, TX; Frank Dally, Ankeny, IA; Sandra England, Kirkland, WA; Ruth Engle, Kirkland, WA; Barbara Fletcher, El Cajon, CA; Paula Foreman, Lancaster, PA; Judy Ginsburgh, Alexandria, LA; Cathy Griffin, Plainsboro, NJ; Peggy Hanley, St. Joseph, MI; Carole Hardy, Pittsburgh, PA; Joan Hunter, Elbridge, NY; Ellen Javernick, Loveland, CO; Wendy Kneeland, Incline Village, NV; Neoma Kreuter, El Dorado Springs, MO; Debra Lindahl, Libertyville, IL; Nancy McAndrew, Shavertown, PA; Judith McNitt, Adrian, MI; Joleen Meier, Wausau, WI; Ruth Miller, San Antonio, TX; Susan Miller, Kutztown, PA; Linda Moenck, Webster City, IA; Donna Mullennix, Thousand Oaks, CA; Natalie Paige, Seattle, WA; Susan Paprocki, Northbrook, IL; Dawn Picolelli, Wilmington, DE; Beverly Qualheim, Marquette, MI; Jane Roake, Oswego, IL; Kay Roozen, Des Moines, IA; Betty Silkunas, Lansdale, PA; Jacki Smallwood, Royersford, PA; Diane Thom, Maple Valley, WA; Margaret Timmons, Fairfield, CT; Becky Valenick, Rockford, IL; Kristine Wagoner, Puyallup, WA; Debbie Wright, Fayette, AR; and Maryann Zucker, Reno, NV.

Editorial Staff
    Editor: Kathleen Cubley
    Contributing Editors: Gayle Bittinger, Jean Warren
    Copy Editor and Proofreader: Kris Fulsaas
    Editorial Assistant: Kate Ffolliott

Design and Production Staff
    Art Manager: Uma Kukathas
    Book Design: Susan Dahlmann
    Book Layout: Sarah Ness
    Cover Design: Brenda Mann Harrison, Susan Dahlman
    Cover Illustration: Susan Dahlmann
    Production Manager: JoAnna Brock

ISBN 1-57029-048-2

Printed in the United States of America
Published by: Warren Publishing House, Inc.
        P.O. Box 2250
        Everett, WA 98203

20 19 18 17 16 15 14 13 12 11 10 9 8 7 6 5 4 3 2 1